My Very Own Organic Cookbook:

The Teen

Book 1

By Frances Rumsey

My Very Own Organic Cookbook: The Teen, Book 1

© 2013 Frances Rumsey

ISBN: 978-1-61170-123-4

RP **Robertson Publishing**™
www.RobertsonPublishing.com

To purchase additional copies of any book in Frances Rumsey's
My Very Own Organic Cookbook series go to:

    amazon.com
    barnesandnoble.com
    www.rp–author.com/rumsey

TABLE OF CONTENTS

Food Chart for Healthy Living

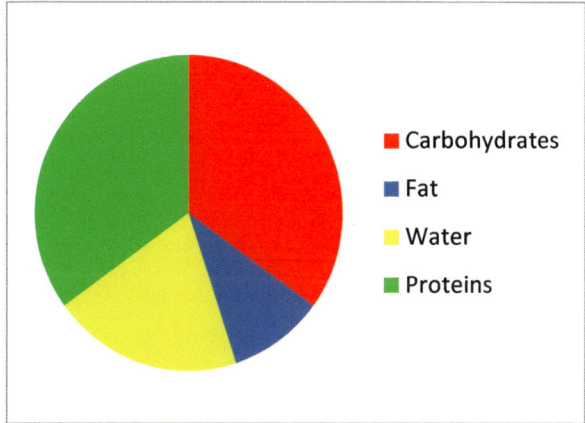

This book is great for any age looking for a healthy and inexpensive way to eat.

FOUR BASIC NUTRIENTS:

Carbohydrates – Supply energy – 35% of your everyday diet

Fat – Support growth and provide energy – 10% of your everyday diet

Water – Hydration – 20% of your everyday diet

Proteins – Make up body tissues, muscles, skin and organs – 35% of your everyday diet

Every child and adult should have at least six meals a day. This means you need to eat around every two hours, starting from the time you get up until the time you go to bed. The servings for each child and adult will depend on the age, size and how active you are. So please keep this in mind when you start your day.

STAY AWAY FROM PROCESSED FOODS: They may include sweeteners, spices, oils, flavors, color, preservatives, nuts, wheat, soy or some form of corn and or milk. This food category is well funded by the government subsidies. **Note:** Wheat, soy, rice, corn, milk, sugar and salt are **fillers** and not part of the Food Chart for Healthy Living.

Exercise Less, Eat More, Lose Weight, and Look Younger!
By Frances Rumsey

I'd like to share some tips to help you keep your body lean and never hungry, the way it was made to be. If you'd like to exercise less, eat more lose weight, and look years younger just follow my tips.

On the *Food Chart for Healthy Living* page in my books there is a guideline to help you choose your foods each day and eat healthy. The guideline details the Four Basic Nutrients that your body needs daily to stay healthy.

Your body needs:

Carbohydrates: 35% of your food intake everyday. Healthy carbs supply your body with the fuel it needs for physical activity and for proper organ function. Carbohydrates are fruit and vegetables only. Stay away from Filler Carbohydrates. These include wheat, soy, rice, corn, milk, sugar and salt. Also stay away from Processed Foods. They may include sweeteners, spices, oils, flavors, color, preservatives, nuts, wheat, soy or some form of corn and/or milk.

Fat: 10% of your food intake everyday. Healthy fats support your heart and support overall health. They are essential to your physical and emotional health, play a huge role in helping you manage your moods, help fight fatigue, and even help control your weight. *NOTE: Fat is better than sugar or salt. I don't recommend fat free because fat free is loaded with sugar and/or salt.*

Proteins: 35% of your food intake everyday. Proteins build up body tissues, muscles, skin and organs. Eating the right amount of protein may improve your level of blood triglycerides and HDL, and may reduce your chances of having a heart attack or stroke.

Water: Your body needs 20% plain water everyday. Every system in your body depends on water. Water supports hydration. Mild dehydration can drain your energy and make you tired. (Note: should not have calorie value, for instance no smoothies or flavored water.)

Every child and adult should have at least six meals a day. Which means you should eat around every two hours. The servings for each child and adult will depend on the age, size and level of activity. So please keep this in mind when you start your day. Eat your first meal as soon as you get up to kick-start your metabolism. Have your last meal shortly before bedtime.

TIPS

1. Choose an amount of calories you need to eat every day. Let's say 1500 calories. *Remember this is an example and everyone will have a different amount of calories they will need.*

2. Divide the calories into six. 1500 divide into six is 250 calories each meal.

3. Now that you have a number for every meal you will need to prepare and plan accordingly.

4. You don't have to wake up at the same time every day and go to bed at the same time every night. You can wake up at 9 am one morning and the next day wake up at 10 am. This will not change or hurt your progress.

5. You MUST eat every two hours. This is very important and will hurt your progress if you don't.

6. You must eat the first meal within 15 minutes of waking up: If you don't your body will stay in a starvation mode until you eat. The moment you eat your first meal your body will let go of any fat it was holding, so eat right away!

7. Once you have your first meal jot down the time. This is important because your two hours starts the moment you've finished the first meal, and so on, on the next meal.

8. The key to this program is reprogramming your body so that it will never go hungry again, even if you decrease the calories. Over time your body will adjust to your new eating schedule.

9. Exercise is important but not essential to this program. 15 minutes twice a day is a good amount and will keep you on track. Remember to eat carbohydrates before you workout for energy and Protein after the workout for repairing the muscles.

10. After a meal and you start to crave sugar, it's your body telling you it needs a digestive enzyme to digest the food you just ate. A lot of digestive enzyme comes in the form of fruit and why the sugar craving comes to you. Grab a fruit or a teaspoon of honey and that will take care of the craving and allow your body to digest and breakdown the food.

11. Substitute sugar for honey and fruit. Substitute salt for garlic and fresh herbs.

12. Allow yourself no more than ¾ teaspoon = 1500 mg sodium a day. And with Sugar allow yourself no more than 3 teaspoons a day. Do not count the natural sugar or salt in fruits and vegetables; that is free. Stay away from all fillers or use a minimum amount (see Food Chart for Healthy Living for a list).

I hope my tips help you become a leaner person. Let the food work for you not against you. You can find fun, easy and healthy ways to cook in any of my organic cookbooks. I'd love to hear from you and the fun you had making my recipes.

Note: Always consult your doctor before changing your diet.

Banana Oatmeal Cookies

INGREDIENTS:

2 organic ripe bananas
1 cup organic quick oats
4 oz of organic apple sauce (see recipe in *My Very Own Organic: Apples*)

DIRECTIONS:

1. Peel and mash bananas in a bowl.
2. Add oats and apple sauce to bowl and mix together until well mixed.
3. Scoop a teaspoon of the mixture onto a cookie sheet, space evenly.

Bake at 350 degrees for about 15 minutes

Broccoli and Bacon Salad

INGREDIENTS:

1 cup fresh organic broccoli tips

¼ cup red onion

¼ cup non-salted cashews

¼ cup cooked bacon (optional)

¼ cup currents

Broccoli and Bacon Salad

DRESSING:

¼ cup fresh organic mayonnaise

1 Tablespoon honey

1 teaspoon white vinegar

1 teaspoon fresh lemon juice

1 teaspoon apple cider vinegar

1 teaspoon dry mustard

DIRECTIONS:

1. Add broccoli tips, red onion, cashews, cooked bacon, and currents to a bowl.
2. In a separate bowl mix mayonnaise, honey white vinegar, lemon juice, apple cider vinegar and dry mustard together.
3. Pour over broccoli mixture. Let everything marinate for 30 minutes in the refrigerator.
4. Served chilled.

Carrot Soup

INGREDIENTS:

1 cup organic carrots
1 cup vegetable broth (see *Vegetable Broth* recipe)
1 garlic clove
1 teaspoon fresh ginger

DIRECTIONS:

1. Peel and cut carrot.
2. Boil carrots and ginger in the vegetable broth until tender.
3. Remove from stove and add garlic.
4. Add everything to blinder, do not over fill blinder. Cover with lid and place towel over lid.
5. Mix until smooth. Serve.

Cauliflower Gratin

INGREDIENTS:

1 cup organic cauliflower

2 Tablespoon organic heavy cream

¼ cup fresh gruyere cheese

¼ cup slivered almonds

DIRECTIONS:

1. Cut and place cauliflower in a baking pan.
2. Pour cream over cauliflower.
3. Sprinkle cheese and almonds over top of cream and cauliflower mixture.

Bake at 350 degrees for 30 minutes or until cauliflower is tender.

Caesar Salad

INGREDIENTS:

10 oz of organic romaine lettuce
½ cup parmesan cheese

DRESSING:

2 anchovy fillets
1 Tablespoon lemon juice
¼ teaspoon Worcestershire sauce
¼ teaspoon mustard
1 egg yolk
¼ cup organic garlic olive oil (see *Infused Garlic Olive Oil* recipe)

Caesar Salad

CROUTONS:

4 slices of French Baguette
2 Tablespoon organic garlic olive oil (see *Infused Garlic Olive Oil* recipe)

DIRECTIONS:

1. Wash, dry then break romaine lettuce into small bite size pieces. Place in a bowl with the parmesan cheese then set aside.
2. In a separate bowl add anchovy fillets. Smash until very fine. Then add lemon juice, Worcestershire sauce, mustard and egg yolk. Mix well. Drizzle garlic olive oil slowly into mixture until well mixed.
3. Pour over romaine lettuce and parmesan cheese salad.
4. Cut baguette slices into small cubes then place on a baking sheet.
5. Drizzle garlic olive oil over cubes and mix together.
6. Bake at 350 degrees for 15 minutes.
7. Let cool then place on top of salad.

Chili/Vegetarian

INGREDIENTS:

16 oz can organic tomatoes (see *My Very Own Organic Cookbook: Tomatoes*)
8 oz can organic tomato sauce (see *My Very Own Organic Cookbook: Tomatoes*)
16 oz can dark red kidney beans
1 cup chopped onion
¾ cup chopped green pepper
4 chopped garlic clove
2 Tablespoon chopped fresh basil
2 teaspoon chili powder

DIRECTIONS:

1. Add tomatoes, tomato sauce, onion, green pepper and garlic in a pot. Let simmer on the medium heat for 20 minutes.
2. Add chili powder, kidney beans and fresh basil. Let simmer on medium heat for another 20 minutes.

Eggplant Rolls

INGREDIENTS:

1 large organic eggplant
1 cup ricotta cheese
1 egg
1 garlic clove
¼ cup parmesan cheese
½ teaspoon salt

MARINARA SAUCE:

1 pint homemade tomatoes sauce (see *My Very Own Organic Cookbook: Tomatoes*)
16 oz can organic tomatoes
1 small chopped onion
1 chopped garlic clove
2 Tablespoon chopped fresh basil
2 Tablespoon organic olive oil

Eggplant Rolls

DIRECTIONS:

1. The eggplant: Cut lengthwise 1/4 –inch slices.
2. Sprinkle salt over eggplant to take out the bitterness of the eggplant.

Bake 350 degrees for 10 minutes until soft and easy to roll.

3. Add Ricotta cheese, egg, garlic in a bowl and mix well.
4. Add a scoop of mixture to each eggplant slice and roll.
5. Place in a pan about 2- inches deep.
6. In a sauce pan add tomatoes chopped onion, garlic, olive oil and fresh basil.
7. Simmer for 20 minutes or until onion is tender.
8. Pour over eggplant.
9. Sprinkle Parmesan cheese over sauce.

Bake at 350 degrees for 30 minutes.

Grilled Artichokes

INGREDIENTS:

1 large organic artichoke
¼ cup organic garlic olive oil (see *Infused Garlic Olive Oil* recipe)

DIRECTIONS:

1. Wash then cut outer leaves short.
2. Boil artichoke for 30 minutes.
3. Then cut artichoke into quarters lengthwise and place on a cookie sheet.
4. Drizzle Infused Garlic Olive Oil over quarters.

Bake at 450 degrees for 30 minutes or until tender.

Granola

INGREDIENTS:

2 cups organic oats

¾ cups almonds

¼ cup organic honey

¾ cup banana chips (see *My Very Own Organic Cookbook: Bananas*)

1 ½ teaspoon pure Vanilla

3 Tablespoons of cinnamon

¼ teaspoon fresh nutmeg

DIRECTIONS:

1. Add all ingredients in a bowl and mix well.
2. Place on a cookie sheet with 1-inch sides. Bake at 275 degrees for 50 minutes. Stir every 10 minutes.

Guacamole

INGREDIENTS:

2 large organic avocadoes
1 small chopped red onion
1 medium chopped organic tomato
1 large chopped garlic clove
1 Tablespoon fresh lemon juice

DIRECTIONS:

1. Peel and mash avocadoes in a bowl. Add chopped onion, chopped tomatoes and garlic. Mash to the consistence desired.
2. Add fresh lemon juice to mixture to stop browning of avocadoes.

Hummus

INGREDIENTS:

15 oz can of chickpeas or garbanzo beans drained and rinsed
1 Tablespoon of juice from the can before draining
1 Tablespoon organic garlic olive oil (see *Infused Garlic Olive Oil* recipe)
¼ teaspoon black pepper or a pinch of cayenne pepper for extra spicy

DIRECTIONS:

1. Mix all the above in a blender and puree until smooth.

Served best with fresh vegetables.

Infused Garlic Olive Oil

INGREDIENTS:

1 cup organic extra virgin olive oil
10 garlic cloves

DIRECTIONS:

1. Add olive oil and garlic into a pot.
2. Bring to a boil then reduce heat to a simmer.
3. Simmer until garlic is golden brown. **Not burnt.**
4. Let cool. Pour into sealed bottles to store, leave a few garlic cloves in bottle to show what it is.

Great for dipping, salad dressings or in cooperate into other dishes.

Leek Soup

INGREDIENTS:

2 medium leeks rinsed and sliced
1 medium carrots peeled and sliced
2 garlic cloves
1 ½ cups of organic vegetable broth (see *Vegetable Broth*
recipe)

DIRECTIONS:

1. Place everything in a pot.
2. Heat to boil. Then reduce heat to simmer for 10. minutes or until vegetables are tender.
3. Pour into a blender. (**Do not over fill**)
4. Puree until smooth.

Oatmeal Apple Scones

INGREDIENTS:

1 ½ cup organic oat flour

2 teaspoons baking powder

1 organic apple peeled and cut into small pieces

2 Tablespoon cinnamon

½ cup apple sauce (see *My Very Own Organic Cookbook: Apples*)

¼ cup organic honey

2 eggs

Oatmeal Apple Scones

DIRECTIONS:

1. Mix flour, baking powder, apple pieces and cinnamon together. Make a well in the middle of the center of the bowl.
2. In another bowl mix apple sauce, honey and an egg together then pour into well of dry ingredients.
3. Pat into dough.
4. Roll out ½ inch thick round.
5. Cut into 8 wedges.

Bake at 350 degrees for 15 minutes or until golden brown.

Pea Soup

INGREDIENTS:

1 cups organic frozen peas
1 ½ cup vegetable broth (see *Vegetable Broth* recipe)
2 garlic cloves

DIRECTIONS:

1. Simmer in a pot for 10 minutes until peas are warmed.
2. Place in a blender (**Do not over fill**).
3. Puree until smooth.

Pumpkin Seeds

INGREDIENTS:

1 cup organic raw pumpkin seeds
¼ teaspoon cayenne pepper (for heat)

DIRECTIONS:

1. Mix all ingredients together then place on a cookie sheet.

Bake at 350 degrees for 20 minutes or until golden brown. Stir every few minutes.

Roasted Vegetable Soup

INGREDIENTS:

1 cup organic tomato sauce (see *My Very Own Organic Cookbook: Tomatoes*)
1 cup organic zucchini
½ cup organic onions
½ cup organic celery
½ cup organic carrots
3 cups organic vegetable broth (see *Vegetable Broth* recipe)
2 Tablespoons fresh parsley
2 Tablespoons fresh basil
2 Tablespoons organic garlic olive oil (see *Infused Garlic Olive Oil* recipe)

Roasted Vegetable Soup

DIRECTIONS:

1. Peel, wash and cut zucchini, onions, celery, and carrots into small pieces.
2. Add to pot with broth, garlic olive oil, parsley and basil.
3. Cook over medium heat for 30 minutes or until vegetables are soft.

Serve as a hearty meal or pour in a blender and puree for a smooth soup.

Rosemary Olive Oil

INGREDIENTS:

1 cup organic extra virgin olive oil
1 full stem of fresh rosemary

DIRECTIONS:

1. Put rosemary and olive oil in a pot.
2. On low heat seep for 30 minutes.
3. Cool then place in a sealed bottle to store.

Spaghetti Squash

INGREDIENTS:

1 medium organic spaghetti squash

DIRECTIONS:

1. Bake at 400 degrees for 1 hour.
2. Let cool then cut lengthwise in half.
3. Remove seeds then pull fork lengthwise separating it into long strands.
4. Add sauce below

Spaghetti Squash

MARINARA SAUCE:

1 pint homemade tomatoes sauce (see *My Very Own Organic Cookbook: Tomatoes*)
16 oz can organic tomatoes
1 small chopped onion
2 Tablespoon chopped fresh basil
2 Tablespoon organic garlic olive oil (see *Infused Garlic Olive Oil*)

DIRECTIONS:

1. Place tomatoes, onion, garlic, basil and olive oil to pan.
2. Simmer on medium heat for 20 minutes or until onions are tender.
3. Pour over spaghetti squash.

Stuffed Jalapenos

INGREDIENTS:

6 organic jalapeno peppers

½ cup mascarpone cheese (Italian cream cheese)

1 chopped garlic clove

1 Tablespoons fresh parsley

DIRECTIONS:

1. Wash then slice the jalapeno lengthwise.
2. Make a boat shape.
3. Scrape seeds out then set aside.
4. Mix cream cheese, garlic, and parsley together.
5. Scoop Tablespoon mixture into each jalapeno.
6. Place on a cookie sheet. Bake at 400 degrees for 25 minutes.

Stuffed Pepper

INGREDIENTS:

2 medium organic peppers (one red and one yellow)
1 small organic zucchini
½ cup ricotta cheese
1 egg
½ cup parmesan cheese
2 garlic cloves

DIRECTIONS:

1. Wash and cut peppers lengthwise and place on a cookie sheet.
2. In a bowl wash and shred zucchini with a grater.
3. Add egg, garlic, ricotta, and parmesan cheese. Stuff peppers. Bake at 350 degrees for 20 minutes.

Trail Mix

INGREDIENTS:

½ cup banana chips (see *My Very Own Organic Cookbook: Bananas*)
¼ cup pumpkin seeds
¼ cup unsweetened coconut
¼ cup sliced almonds
¼ cup dried cranberries
¼ cup raisins

DIRECTIONS:

1. Mix the above in a bowl.
2. Store in plastic bags.

Vegetable Broth

INGREDIENTS:

1 organic onion
4 stems of organic celery sticks
2 organic carrots
16 oz can organic tomatoes or (see *My Very Own Organic Cookbook: Tomatoes*)
5 garlic cloves
1 handful of fresh parsley

DIRECTIONS:

1. Add the above in a pot.
2. Simmer on medium heat for 2 hours.
3. Strain, then when cool enough store in a plastic container.

Vegetable (No Pasta) Lasagna

INGREDIENTS:

2 medium organic butternut squash

1 cup organic baby spinach

15 oz ricotta cheese

4 garlic cloves

2 Tablespoons fresh parsley

1 egg

1 cup parmesan cheese

10 oz mozzarella cheese

Vegetable (No Pasta) Lasagna

MARINARA SAUCE:

1 pint homemade tomatoes sauce (see *My Very Own Organic Cookbook: Tomatoes*)

16 oz can organic tomatoes

1 small chopped onion

2 Tablespoon chopped fresh basil

2 Tablespoon organic garlic olive oil (see *Infused Garlic Olive Oil*)

DIRECTIONS:

1. Bake butternut squash whole at 350 degrees for 40 minutes until almost cooked through.
2. Set aside and let cool.
3. In a bowl mix ricotta, garlic, egg, fresh parsley and parmesan cheese together.
4. When butternut squash is cool, peel and slice lengthwise ¼ inch thick.
5. In a 2 inch deep baking pan pour some sauce on bottom of pan.
6. Place butternut squash slices over sauce. Add ricotta mixture over butternut squash then add spinach and mozzarella.
7. Keep layering until butternut squash is on top. Then add some sauce over that.

Bake at 350 degrees for 60 minutes. Let set for 15 minutes before serving.

CPSIA information can be obtained
at www.ICGtesting.com
Printed in the USA
LVIC080627170513
334039LV00006B